Design

↓ *Admiral Graf Spee* at Kiel, just prior to the outbreak of the Second World War.

THE establishment of a provisional *Reichsmarine* in April 1919 provided the framework for a revived German Navy after the traumas of the First World War. The Treaty of Versailles, the terms of which were published in May 1919 (and to which the German signature was appended the following month) had an immediate and violent effect with the ordering by *Vizeadmiral* Ludwig von Reuter that the High Seas Fleet—the bulk of which was lying interned in foreign waters— be scuttled in order to avoid the ignominy associated with reparations.

Unrest and political turmoil, simmering at the close of hostilities (particularly in the Navy, which since Jutland had been for the most part idling its time away in port), spread quickly after the Armistice, and was fanned by the harsh terms of the Treaty. The result was catastrophic for a once-proud service: its major ships had been either confiscated or were lying at the bottom of Scapa Flow, its hierarchy was in chaos, and its personnel were totally disillusioned.

In terms of assets, the *Reichsmarine* was but a shadow of its former self. Its largest front-line vessels were now six obsolete pre-dreadnoughts each equipped with four 28cm guns, and half a dozen light cruisers whose design dated back to the nineteenth century. However, the limits placed on the establishment meant that, in any case, only a small fraction of the available ships could be in commission at any one time: with no more than

15,000 personnel permitted, there were simply not enough able bodies to man what remained. The restrictions imposed by the Treaty, moreover, prevented replacements being brought into service for some years, and limited what could be built at that time to a displacement of 10,000 tons: the theory was that even a revitalised German Navy would not be able to commission anything bigger than a coast-defence battleship.

In the meantime, the Washington Treaty of 1922 had imposed building restrictions on the five major navies of the world (and therefore, by default, on every other navy too). As regards capital ships, the limits place on gun calibre (16in) hardly affected Germany, since her displacement limits were in force. However, in the matter of cruisers, there was more room for manoeuvre. The Treaty stipulated a maximum displacement of 10,000 tons—i.e., the same as that imposed on Germany for all her ships—and a maximum calibre of 8in. The Treaty was, it must be stressed, only of incidental interest to German naval architects since they had their own constraints within which to work; moreover, Germany was not a signatory to the Washington agreement, and therefore, even if it had had practical application, would not have been bound by it.

Panzerschiffe

Naval architects always have to work within constraints—physical and fin-

Panzerschiffe: Preliminary Designs, March 1927

Design	Displacement (tons)	Armament	Armour (mm)	Speed (kt)
A	10,000	4 x 38cm	250	18
B1	10,000	6 x 30.5cm	250	18
B2	10,000	6 x 30.5cm	200	21
C	10,000	6 x 28cm	100	26–27

ancial—and their task is to arrive at the best possible compromise solution that will fulfil the role or roles intended. The restrictions placed on German naval construction were of course very great, and as well as posing problems they offered scope for ingenuity. The 'big ships' that did appear were unique: they were neither battleships nor cruisers, yet at the same time they incorporated traditional features of both types.

Light cruisers and torpedo-boats took priority in the new *Reichsmarine*: they represented the most effective use of the resources and personnel available and, moreover, were the types in most urgent need of replacement, were less costly than heavier units and could be taken into service fairly rapidly. The dilemma facing the designers of the replacement ships for the pre-dreadnoughts was severe. On a displacement of only 10,000 tons, it was not at all obvious whether any sort of battleship-type gun calibre could be installed.

A large number of sketch designs were produced, culminating in 1927

▼ *Deutschland* on trials, early 1933, bereft of a great deal of her equipment.

↑ *Deutschland,
probably in the spring
of 1936.*

in a formal submission to the C-in-C
Naval Command, Admiral Zenker (see
accompanying table). The classic
trade-offs were there, writ large: maximum calibre, maximum armour or
maximum speed? Zenker decided in
favour of speed, with the result that
armament and armour were sacrifced.
The design went further: it was to incorporate diesel machinery, not merely
for cruising as had been the case in
the 'K' class cruisers, but as the main
power source. The risks inherent in
relying on this relatively novel form of
propulsion were accepted in the interests of the great range it would confer
on the new vessels. The 28cm gun was
adopted primarily because it had a
good track record in German service,
its characteristics were known, and its
ammunition was of proven capability.

Design Details

The hull was built on the normal longi-
tudinal bulkhead and transverse

frame principle, with welded seams,
the latter having proved satisfactory
during the First World War and also
offering a marked saving in weight—
some 15 per cent—over the more usual
rivetted construction. The armour belt
was inclined, and designed to defeat
projectiles fired from cruisers; it was
80mm amidships at its maximum,
with a 50mm strake at the base, below
the waterline, tapering to 60mm and
then 50–30mm aft and 10mm forward,
and supplemented by a 45mm (maximum) torpedo bulkhead inboard of
the main belt and 40mm armoured
bulkheads inboard between the armoured deck and the upper deck. Horizontal protection comprised the 30mm
armoured deck inboard across the
citadel, thickening to 45mm outboard
although the latter extended only as
far as the inboard inclined bulkhead.

The main armament was disposed
in two triple turrets—the first time this
arrangement had been seriously con-
sidered for the German Navy. The
choice of triples cut down ship length
and thus saved weight, and two triples
were in themselves less weighty than
three twins. The calibre of the guns
was actually 28.3cm, and the barrels,
although developed from the First
World War design as shipped aboard
the battlecruisers *Moltke* and *Seydlitz*,
were radically different from, and con-
siderably lighter than, their predec-
essors of twenty years before.

The 15cm gun was a relatively new
weapon, developed from the C16

Panzerschiffe: Outline Legend, April 1928	
Displacement:	10,000 tons
Dimensions:	Length 185.7m overall, 181.7m waterline; beam 20.5m maximum, 20.0m waterline; draught 5.77m
Armament:	6 x 28cm L/50 (2 x 3); 8 x 15cm L/55 (8 x 1); 3 x 8.8cm L/75 (3 x 1); 4 x 3.7cm L/83 (2 x 2); 6 x 53.3cm torpedo tubes (2 x 3)
Machinery:	Diesel, two shafts (54,000bhp per shaft)
Speed:	26kt
Range:	17,500nm at 13kt, 16,500nm at 14kt, 10,000nm at 20kt

Panzerschiffe: Armament Details, as designed

	Main	Sec	Heavy AA	Light AA
Calibre (cm)	28	15	8.8*	3.7
Mounting type	C28	C28	C13	C30
Barrel length (cal)	52.35	55	76	83
Muzzle velocity (m/s)	910	875	790	1,000
Maximum range (km)	36.5	22.0	15.5	8.5†
Elevation/depression (°)	+40/–10	+35/–10	+70/–10	+85/–10
Rate of fire (rds/min)	2	10	n/a	160‡
Weight of projectile (kg)	300	45.3	9	0.74
Supply (rds/gun)	105–120	100–150	n/a	n/a

* This particular model was only fitted in *Deutschland*.
† In surface mode.
‡ Theoretical; in practice, the rate of fire was less than half this figure.

model of the First World War; it had already been fitted to the 'K' class light cruisers and would go on to equip the *Scharnhorst* and *Bismarck* class battleships. The 8.8cm was primarily an anti-aircraft weapon but was extremely useful against surface targets too. The C13 model was an ancient weapon and was swiftly replaced in service by the later C32; indeed, only the first ship of the class ever carried it. Eight semi-automatic C30 3.7cm light AA weapons were stipulated, disposed in twin mountings abreast the forward and after superstructure.

Eight torpedo tubes were mounted in quadruple banks either side of the quarterdeck, close to the deck-edge and well forward. The original design included 50cm tubes, but only the first ship was so fitted, and these were swiftly relinquished in favour of the standard 53.3cm model.

From the start, the class was designed to operate spotter aircraft, two of which would be carried, with a turntable catapult amidships.

Fire control for the main armament was regulated by means of two 10.5m rangefinders, one at the foretop and one on the after superstructure, with 10.5m rangefinders for local control at each turret; a 7m rangefinder forward of the bridge for 15cm control; and two 3m rangefinders for AA control, one forward and one aft.

The diesel propulsion system for the class was something of a novelty, and the choice was not without risk. Development of marine diesels started in Germany before the First World War, and there were plans to fit some of the *Reichsmarine*'s capital ships with centre-shaft diesels, complementing the turbines used for the outer shafts. These came to naught, but development continued, and in the mid-1920s suitable powerplants were available for installation in German light cruisers—albeit only as auxiliary propulsion. By 1927 development had reached the point where reliability suitable for primary installation was acceptable, coinciding with the design phase of the German *Panzerschiffe*. The arrangement comprised eight MAN M9Z42/58 9-cylinder, double-acting two-stroke engines disposed as two sets, each driving a 4m propeller, each motor producing some 7,000bhp for a maximum shaft speed of 250rpm.

The advantages of diesel propulsion were many: power for the ship was immediately available when required; the absence of any necessity for boilers, and the savings in personnel and space that this conferred; more compact, if heavy, machinery units; and, above all, fuel economy, offering, if required, great range. There can be no doubt that the principal reason for the choice of diesels for these ships was

➡ Two views of *Admiral Graf Spee* fitting out at Wilhelmshaven, 1935.

Deutschland Class					
	Builder	Laid down	Launched	Commissioned	Cost (RM)
Deutschland	Deutsche Werke, Kiel	5 Feb 1929	19 May 1931	1 Apr 1933	80.0
Admiral Scheer	Marinewerft, Wilhelmshaven	25 Jun 1931	1 Apr 1933	12 Nov 1934	90.0
Admiral Graf Spee	Marinewerft, Wilhelmshaven	1 Oct 1932	30 Jun 1934	6 Jan 1936	82.0

their envisaged role as commerce raiders.

Design Differences

The three ships of the class—named *Deutschland* class after the first to be launched—exhibited considerable detail differences, not surprisingly in view of the substantial gaps between their keel-laying dates. The most obvious difference concerned the design of the forward superstructure. The original layout comprised a tubular, pole-like *Turmmast* ('tower

← *Deutschland* just prior to her commissioning, 1 April 1933. The torpedo tubes are lacking their protective shields.

↓ *Scheer* making gentle way, 1936. The original design of the *Turmmast*, which differed radically from that fitted aboard *Deutschland*, is clearly seen.

mast'), but only *Deutschland* retained this; by the time the two later ships appeared it had been replaced by a more substantial, tapered structure with enclosed decks. Less obviously, it should be noted that *Deutschland's* bridge structure and funnel were positioned marginally further forward than on her two sisters.

The armament specifications differed amongst the ships: *Deutschland* commissioned with the C13 model 8.8cm (single mounting) whereas *Scheer* received the improved C25 model (twin); *Graf Spee* commissioned with 10.5cm AA in place of the 8.8cm (three twin mountings, virtually identical to those for the C13 8.8cm). The aircraft catapult eventually fitted was sited between foremast and funnel in

Deutschland but abaft the funnel in her sister-ships, and the name-ship also completed without a mainmast, whereas *Scheer* and *Graf Spee* featured a light pole affixed to the after contours of the funnel, with an associated platform at approximately three-quarters the height of the funnel. The design of the handling derricks abreast and immediately abaft the funnel also differed. Upon commissioning, *Graf Spee* could be readily distinguished from *Scheer* in having her foremast braced at a distance from the *Turmmast* rather than adjacent to it, and she also sported light tripod legs to her mainmast. For a short time after the ship's commissioning, *Deutschland's* torpedo tubes lacked their armoured shielding.

Careers

THE appearance of these hybrid vessels took the world by surprise, and initial reactions were mixed. They did not fall neatly into any existing category of fighting ship, and much Press comment of the day was derisory: with a displacement of 'only' 10,000 tons and an armament of 'only' six 28cm (11in) guns, they were ridiculed by some British journalists, who immediately nicknamed them 'pocket battleships'. Wiser heads were more cautious. It was known that they had diesel powerplants (the details were, however, closely guarded), conferring great range: clearly, the ships were in reality cruisers, and very powerfully armed at that. The message was obvious: in time of war, they could, if allowed to break out, wreak havoc amongst the merchant shipping routes.

So concerned were the Admiralty in Britain and the Ministère de la Marine in France that ways in which a response could be made were the subject of high-level talks between the two national governments. The only faster and more heavily armed ships on either's inventory were the three British battlecruisers, *Hood*, *Repulse* and *Renown*; the French had nothing that could outrun them except much more lightly armed cruisers. It is generally held that the French, still fearful of a resurgent Germany, laid down her two *Dunkerque* class battleships as a response to the *Deutschlands*; Britain, having just commissioned the two *Nelson*s—a good 6 knots slower than the *Panzerschiffe*—had no tonnage available to build new capital ships owing to the constraints of the Washington Treaty.

➡ *Deutschland* at Hamburg, 28 May 1934.

DEUTSCHLAND

The first operational commitment for all three ships arose out of the Spanish Civil War, wherein a number of European navies maintained 'neutrality patrols' and assisted in the evacuation of nationals and refugees after hostilities broke out on 17 July 1936.

Deutschland made five such tours of duty: July–August and October–November 1936, January–March and May–June 1937, and October 1937–February 1938. The ship saw action for the first time during the fourth tour, when in the evening of 29 May, off Ibiza, she was approached by a force of Spanish Republican cruisers and destroyers, which immediately took steps to engage, while at the same time two Republican aircraft attacked from the north-west. The shells fell short, but the aircraft were more successful, two bombs striking the ship. The first landed on the starboard side amidships, close to one of the 15cm mountings, setting off a petrol fire which destroyed the ship's aircraft and consumed one of the ship's boats. The second hit was much more serious. It penetrated the upper deck in the region of 'A' turret, the subsequent explosion and fire killing or injuring the entire turret crew and venting through the *Turmmast*. In all, *Deutschland* suffered 141 casualties, 31 fatal, and was compelled to return to Wilhelmshaven.

First Shots—and a New Name

On 24 August 1939 *Deutschland* took on ammunition, left Wilhelmshaven and, six days later, met up with her assigned tanker, *Westerwald*, off Cape Farewell at the southern tip of Greenland. On 27 September she received authorisation to begin anti-commerce operations, and by the 30th she was hunting for victims plying the route between Bermuda and the Azores.

Her first success was scored, against the 5,000-ton *Stonegate*, on 5 October, whereupon the ship moved north and on the 9th, off Newfoundland, came upon the the US freighter *City of Flint*, which, suspected of carrying contraband, was promptly seized. In a bizarre series of twists, the American ship, with the *Stonegate*'s crew on board, was taken to Norway by a prize captain put aboard by *Deutschland*, but the German prize crew were arrested by the Norwegian authorities and the freighter returned to US custody.

The Norwegian freighter *Lorentz W. Hansen* was sunk off Newfoundland on 14 October, but within a couple of weeks bad weather forced an early return to Germany to repair storm damage, and on 16 November *Deutschland* arrived in Gotenhafen. By this time it had become known aboard that the ship was to be given a new name—*Lützow*. The widely published story that Hitler, whose faith in the *Kriegsmarine* was never entirely wholehearted, could not countenance the

◄The effect of the a Republican bomb dropped on *Deutschland*, 29 May 1937, which burnt out the ship's Heinkel He 60 spotter aircraft.

↑ *Deutschland* on her return to Germany for repairs, June 1937. Neutrality stripes (red, white and black; red forward) are painted across 'A' turret.

loss of a ship bearing the name of the Fatherland is not without foundation, but a more compelling reason is that *Grossadmiral* Raeder, the C-in-C of the Navy wished to confuse enemy intelligence, especially as the sale of *Hipper* class heavy cruiser named *Lützow* was the subject of negotiations with the Soviet Union at that time. A public announcement was made on 15 February 1940, when it was also revealed that the *Panzerschiffe* had officially been reclassified as heavy cruisers.

Norwegian Watch

The German invasion of Norway got under way on 7 April 1940, and *Lützow* (as she was now named) was assigned to *Gruppe 5*, bound for Oslo, in company with the ill-fated heavy cruiser *Blücher*, the light cruiser *Emden*, three torpedo boats and assorted minesweepers and smaller vessels. On board were 450 troops of the German occupation forces. Entering the Drö-bak Narrows, Oslofjord, in the evening of 8 April, with *Blücher* leading, the German force quickly came under concentrated fire from Norwegian shore batteries. *Blücher* was hit repeatedly and succumbed the following morning; *Lützow* was hit three times by 15cm

shells and also struck by smaller-calibre fire, but managed to extricate herself without major damage. 'A' turret was hit and put out of action for half an hour; the second pierced the hull (via a scuttle) and caused damage and injuries in the ship's sick bay; and the third struck home on the port side abreast the funnel, causing the port crane and spotter aircraft abaft the funnel to be put out of action and casualties amongst the port after 15cm gun crews.

Worse was to follow, however. On 11 April, en route for Kiel, *Lützow* was torpedoed by the British submarine *Spearfish*, and almost lost her stern as a result. She was towed into port three days later, and the extent of the repairs required put her out of commission for almost a year.

Lützow's second foray into the Atlantic shipping lanes had long been planned, and the successes scored by *Scharnhorst* and *Gneisenau* earlier in the year gave further encouragement to the *Seekriegsleitung*. However, following the loss of the battleship *Bismarck* on 27 May 1941, the policy of sending surface raiders out on such sorties came under close scrutiny. Nevertheless, it was decided to send

9

Lützow out, and on 12 June she moved from Kiel to Norway for Operation 'Sommerreise'. She got no further: at about midnight she was attacked by a Beaufort torpedo-bomber of No 42 Squadron RAF. The weapon hit the cruiser amidships on the port side, knocking out her engines and electrical power and flooding several compartments.

Once again, the damage was serious, but the ship managed to return to Kiel under her own power. Repairs would take until January 1942 to complete. Thus far, *Deutschland/Lützow*'s war career had been far from glowing. In two and a half years of conflict, she had spent all but about six months undergoing repairs as a result of en-emy action, and her sole successes had been been two merchant ships sunk. She moved to Norway in May 1942, but achieved very little of practical significance and returned to Kiel for minor repairs in August. In November she returned to Norway once more, surviving air attacks en route to Altafjord, where she made fast.

In Operation 'Regenbogen', a German attack on the Allied Arctic convoy JW.51B involving the heavy cruisers *Admiral Hipper* and *Lützow* and destroyers, she managed to make contact on 31 December and inflict severe damage on the destroyer HMS *Obdurate*, one of the escorts. Despite this, the operation was swiftly called off by the German commander of the task

⬆⬆ *Lützow* (ex *Deutschland*) down at the stern after being torpedoed in the Skagerrak on her way home from 'Weserübung', the German invasion of Norway. Note the two Arado 196 floatplanes, that forward sitting atop the catapult.
⬆ *Lützow* in April 1941 in her striking black-and-white dazzle camouflage scheme.

10

↑ *Lützow* back in Baltic waters, winter 1944/45, with a pristine paint scheme, 15cm guns trained abeam and additional light AA weapons installed (note, for example, the 2cm single mounting on the forepeak).

↓ *Lützow*'s final days at Swinemünde.

group following orders from Command Headquarters ashore not to expose his ships to unnecessary risk—whatever that might have meant.

Following this fiasco, Hitler issued his famous *Führerordnung* requiring the decommissioning of all the *Kriegsmarine*'s heavy ships. Raeder resigned in protest, his place being taken by *Grossadmiral* Karl Dönitz, erstwhile head of the U-Boat Arm. Dönitz's powers of persuasion resulted in some relaxing of the decommissioning order, but *Lützow* continued to languish uselessly in the Norwegian fjords for another eight months. She returned to Germany unscathed in September 1943, went into refit, and did not emerge until the following February.

Baltic Finale

Lützow spent the rest of her career in the Baltic, supporting the retreating German forces as they were pushed back ever further by the Soviet onslaught from the east. She was in place to support Operation 'Tanne West', the German occupation of the Aaland Islands, in June 1944, but this undertaking proved abortive. In October, together with the heavy cruiser *Prinz Eugen* and destroyers, she covered the evacuation of Estonia, and later that month she bombarded Soviet positions

around Memel in Lithuania in the face of severe air attacks. February and March saw *Lützow* off East Prussia, supporting the German Fourth Army as it tried to stem the inexorable Soviet advance.

Her final voyage ended on 8 April 1945, when, as she had done periodically, she put into Swinemünde to replenish ammunition. Eight days later, during an RAF raid, she had her hull gashed by a near-miss from a 10,000lb bomb, quickly took on water and listed. However, her fighting days were not quite over. 'A' turret and some of her secondary battery were pumped out, power was restored, and *Lützow* resumed her shelling of the approaching Soviet forces. Eventually her ammunition was exhausted, and, together with the old battleship *Schleswig-Holstein* and other vessels at the port, she was blown up. The fate of her wreck is not known.

ADMIRAL SCHEER

Admiral Scheer joined her sister-ship *Deutschland* for a tour of duty following the outbreak of the Spanish Civil War, both ships leaving Wilhelmshaven on 24 July 1936, but both this and the second and third tours (2 October–3 December 1936 and 15 March–7 April 1937) proved uneventful.

The ship's first taste of action came on the next occasion she was despatched to Spanish waters (9 May–1 July 1937): in response to the Republican bombing attack on *Deutschland* (q.v.), she opened fire with all three calibres on shore installations at Almeria on 31 May and caused extensive damage and casualties.

Three more tours of duty were completed (30 July–11 October 1937, 12 February–14 March 1938 and 19 March–29 June 1938), but, other than the usual exercises, war watches and patrols, very little of significance occurred.

Ocean Raider

Admiral Scheer spent the first months of the Second World War at Wilhelmshaven and exercising in the Baltic, but on 1 February 1940 she was taken in hand for a thorough refit, recommis-

Admiral Scheer dressed overall, 1936.

↑ *Admiral Scheer* in 1939, now with new platforms either side of the *Turmmast* and with gaffs added to the mainmast.

sioning on 31 July much altered in appearance.

After working up, she left Gotenhafen on 23 October that year, met up with her oiler *Nordmark* and eight days later, having eluded detection by British forces, made her way through the Denmark Strait and into the North Atlantic, where she encountered the eastbound convoy HX.24 and proceeded to wreak havoc. Nine merchantmen fell victim, six of them, including the armed merchant cruiser *Jervis Bay*, sinking as a result. She then moved to the West Indies, replen-

ishing her bunkers and sinking another ship before moving to the area of the Canaries, where the *Tribesman* succumbed. The remainder of the cruise took her into the Indian Ocean, north of Madagascar, where she found further trade. She somehow managed to elude the Royal Navy throughout her voyage, and she returned through the Denmark Strait once more to a triumphant welcome in Kiel.

By the time she had been made ready for a second foray into the trade routes in the summer of 1941, the policy of sending heavy surface war-

---

Admiral Scheer: Merchantmen sunk and captured, 1940–41

Date	Ship	Tonnage	Nationality	Remarks
5 Nov 1940	*Mopan*	5,389	British	Sunk
5 Nov 1940	*Jervis Bay*	14,6164	British	Convoy HX.84; sunk
5 Nov 1940	*Maidan*	7,908	British	Convoy HX.84; sunk
5 Nov 1940	*Trewellard*	5,201	British	Convoy HX.84; sunk
5 Nov 1940	*Beaverford*	10,042	British	Convoy HX.84; sunk
5 Nov 1940	*Kanbane Head*	5,225	British	Convoy HX.84; sunk
5 Nov 1940	*Fresno City*	4,955	British	Convoy HX.84; sunk
24 Nov 1940	*Port Hobart*	7,448	British	Sunk
1 Dec 1940	*Tribesman*	6,242	British	Sunk
18 Dec 1940	*Duquesa*	8,561	British	Prize
18 Jan 1941	*Sandefjord*	10,000	British	Prize
19 Jan 1941	*Barneveld*	5,200	Dutch	Prize
19 Jan 1941	*Stanpark*	5,600	British	Sunk
20 Feb 1941	*British Advocate*	6,994	British	Prize
21 Feb 1941	*Gregorios C II*	2,546	Greek	Sunk
21 Feb 1941	*Canadian Cruiser*	7,178	Canadian	Sunk
22 Feb 1941	*Rantaupandjang*	2,542	Dutch	Sunk

Mopan and the victims of HX-84 were despatched in the North Atlantic, *Port Hobart* and *Tribesman* in the Central Atlantic, the next four in the South Atlantic and the final four in the southern Indian Ocean. As well as the sinkings, three ships from HX.84 were damaged.

ships into the Atlantic was being re-assessed in the light of the *Bismarck* disaster, and, apart from a brief visit to Oslo, where she managed to dodge the attentions of RAF bomber crews, she spent the next six months either at Kiel or in the Baltic, keeping a watchful eye on the Russian fleet while 'Barbarossa', Hitler's invasion of the Soviet Union, developed.

'Rösselsprung', 'Wunderland'

Seeing little possibility of further success on the Atlantic trade routes, the *Seekriegsleitung* cast around for ways in which the heavy ships of the German Navy could be most usefully employed. The obvious place to which they could best be deployed was Norway: here there were scores of natural anchorages, well protected from prying eyes by the steep slopes of the mountains surrounding the fjords, and close to the growing Arctic convoy traffic taking essential supplies and war materials to the Soviet Union. Furthermore, the threat alone under which the convoys would be placed would be such as to prompt a considerable de-ployment of British resources which otherwise could be directed at Germany elsewhere.

Scheer and her sister-ship *Lützow*, along with the battleship *Tirpitz*, the heavy cruiser *Admiral Hipper* and numerous smaller combatants, now formed a battle group based in Norway, the two former pocket-battleships making up Force II based at Narvik. Her first hostile sortie—as part of Operation 'Rösselsprung', an all-out attack on convoy PQ.17 sailing from Reykjavik to northern Russia—proved a total fiasco as all the heavy ships were recalled to base before they could get among the merchantmen, the risk of being engaged by Allied warships being judged too great. Meanwhile the Luftwaffe and the U-boat arm had great success, sinking two dozen ships with equal honours.

One further operation took place in 1942 when in August *Scheer* rounded the North Cape, sailed into the Barents Sea, passed Cape Zhelaniye and continued into the Kara Sea with a view to disrupting shipping and attacking shore installations. The ice-

◄ *Admiral Scheer* in Bogen Bay, near Narvik, during the ship's long sojourn in Norwegian waters. The air recognition swastika on the foredeck has been covered.
➡ *Scheer* close up amidships in late 1944, showing the single FuMO 26 antenna at the foretop and the second funnel modification—a further increase to the rake to the cap. The twin 10.5cm mounting abreast the funnel has been draped over.

breaker *Alexander Sibiryakov* was spotted and sunk, whereupon *Scheer* sailed for Port Dickson and bombarded the harbour there. She arrived back in Narvik on 30 August.

By the end of the year the ship was at Wilhelmshaven for refit, during which she received some splinter damage during an air raid on 26 February 1943.

The Final Years

Admiral Scheer's last two years of service complemented that of her one remaining sister-ship: with Allied supremacy established in the west and with the relentless Soviet advance getting under way in the east, and with shortages of fuel and ammunition beginning to take effect, Germany's surface fleet was all but bottled up in the Baltic. There was little opportunity for aggressive operations, and a good deal of time was spent schooling cadets, batches of 500 at a time being embarked for seamanship training.

On 22 November 1944 the cruiser sailed for the Sworbe peninsula to bombard Soviet positions in an attempt to relieve the pressure on the retreating German land forces, and in February and March the following year she was off East Prussia doing much the same job. By 18 March 1945 she was back at Kiel for re-ammunitioning.

Her end was near. On 9 April there was a devastatingly heavy air raid on Kiel, and *Scheer* was hit and near-missed by a rain of bombs. The order was given to abandon ship, and she quickly capsized, trapping several crewmen below decks.

Later that summer, after the capitulation, the wreck was ordered to be broken up by the British authorities and the hulk was abandoned.

ADMIRAL GRAF SPEE

Of the three pocket battleships operated by the *Kriegsmarine*, *Admiral Graf Spee* is the best known and also had the shortest career: hardly had the Second World War broken out than she was at large, sinking ships in the Atlantic, but before 1939 was out she had been brought to action, and had gone down in an inglorious finale. At

the start of the war, she was already well known to the British public, having received considerable Press coverage during her symbolic attendance at the Naval Review to mark the coronation of King George VI.

Deployment

Graf Spee made five deployments to Spanish waters during the time of the Spanish Civil War (20 August–9 October 1936, 13 December 1936–14 February 1937, 2 March–6 May and 23 June–7 August 1937, and 7–18 February 1938), but she saw no hostile action and came through her experiences unscathed.

When the Second World War broke out on 1 September 1939, *Graf Spee*, like her sister-ship *Deutschland*, was already in the Atlantic, fully provisioned, fuelled and armed for anti-commerce operations. The fleet tanker *Altmark*, *Graf Spee*'s replenishment ship, had earlier filled her bunkers in the United States and joined her. The two vessels would meet up on several occasions over the next four months as *Graf Spee* conducted her campaign in the mid-Atlantic and Indian Oceans.

The go-ahead for operations was given on 26 September, and within four days the first success had been achieved when the merchantman *Clement* was sunk off Brazil. Eight

more ships were accounted for over the next eleven weeks.

From 5 October, British and French forces were assembled in considerable strength in an effort to bring *Graf Spee* to bay, individual hunting groups being established in the West Indies, the Bay of Biscay, the Cape Town area, off West Africa, off the coast of South America and in the Indian Ocean, the last drawing in additional forces when news broke in mid-November that the enemy was oper-

↑ A prewar view of *Graf Spee*'s stern showing the anchor and emblem.
↓ Another prewar photograph of *Graf Spee*, with He 60 spotter plane atop the catapult.

↑ *Graf Spee* was similar in appearance to *Scheer*, but her foremast was deeper and the mainmast sported tripod legs.

ating off Madagascar. Battleships, battlecruisers, aircraft carriers, heavy and light cruisers and smaller warships were all involved, so great was the fear of what this potent surface raider might achieve while still at large.

She was discovered on 13 December off the coast of Uruguay by a group comprising the heavy cruiser *Exeter* and the light cruisers *Ajax* and *Achilles*—the last a New Zealand vessel with the group commander, Commodore Harwood, on board—and what would prove to be one of the classic naval actions of the Second World War quickly developed. The three cruisers

split into two groups, *Exeter* approaching from the south on her own while the two 6in-gun cruisers sped eastward in an attempt to circle *Graf Spee* from the north, and thus the German vessel was from the start forced to divide her fire. Nevertheless, excellent gunnery inflicted severe damage on two of the enemy, *Exeter* being all but knocked out of action and only *Achilles* escaping with light damage and casualties. However, *Graf Spee* had herself suffered, and although her armament was unaffected she was low on 28cm ammunition and much of her plant needed repair.

***Admiral Graf Spee*: Merchantmen sunk and captured, 1939**

Date	Ship	Tonnage	Nationality	Remarks
30 Sep 1939	*Clement*	5,051	British	Sunk
5 Oct 1939	*Newton Beech*	4,651	British	Prize, then sunk
7 Oct 1939	*Ashlea*	4,222	British	Sunk
9 Oct 1939	*Huntsman*	8,196	British	Prize, then sunk
22 Oct 1939	*Trevanion*	5,299	British	Sunk
15 Nov 1939	*Africa Shell*	706	British	Sunk
2 Dec 1939	*Doric Star*	10,086	British	Sunk
2 Dec 1939	*Tairoa*	7,983	British	Sunk
7 Dec 1939	*Streonshalh*	3,895	British	Sunk

All were sunk in the Central Atlantic except *African Shell*, which fell victim off Mozambique.

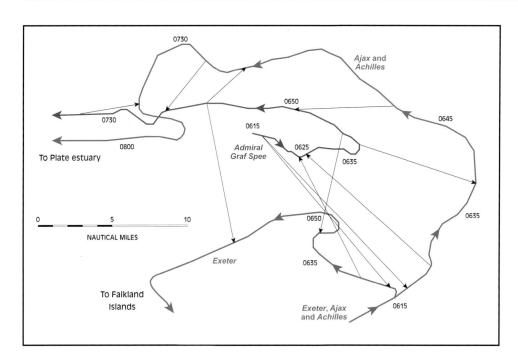

◀ The main action at the Battle of the River Plate, 13 December 1939.
▮ The end: smoke billows as *Graf Spee* takes fire after scuttling charges have been detonated.

Her captain, *Kapitän zur See* Langsdorff, decided to make for the neutral port of Montevideo in order to make his ship seaworthy, but under international law he could remain there for three days only, Uruguay being a neutral and Germany a belligerent state. His hosts might possibly be persuaded to allow him the extra time he so sorely needed, but by the time he finished there could be little doubt that further British forces would have been brought up, awaiting his departure. He therefore decided to scuttle the ship, and at 1830 on 17 December *Graf Spee* made her last, six-mile voyage out into the River Plate and the skeleton crew set off their scuttling charges. Violent explosions and huge clouds of smoke followed, and at about 2100 the most famous of the three pocket-battleships sank.

Model Products

➡➡ Clydeside Models *Admiral Graf Spee*, to 1/1200 scale.

Interest in German military operations during the Second World War continues even sixty years after the events took place, and this, together with the fact that the weapons of war used in these operations are very well documented, ensures that models relating to the period remain very popular indeed. The plastic kit manufacturers recognise a profitable investment when they see one, and the result is that the *Kriegsmarine* is extremely well represented. Apart from, perhaps, the light cruisers, virtually all the major German warships that participated in the conflict can be found in their catalogues—few lack a *Bismarck* or a *Scharnhorst*—while U-boats are also well represented, and there are some excellent large-scale models of S-boats.

The pocket-battleships are there in strength, ranging in scale from 1/400 down to 1/700 together with a selection of offerings in smaller scales to cater for the wargamer. The most salesworthy is of course *Admiral Graf Spee*—one of the half-dozen or so warship names from the Second World War with which almost everyone will be familiar—but there are kits for her two sister-ships too; moreover, although the class members differed significantly in appearance from one another, the degree of commonality was such that any one of them can fairly readily be modelled from a kit representing either of the others. The exact close-range weapons fits of the two survivors in the last desperate months of the war are the subject of continuing discussion, but the class as a whole offers not only interesting possibilities for the creative model-maker who likes to stamp his own imprint on his work, but also a variety of different liveries and camouflage schemes for those whose talents lie instead, or also, with the paintbrush.

The 'after-market' accessory manufacturers also offer a variety of fixtures and fittings to enable the model-maker to enhance his work, although, in general, class-specific packages are not on offer: recourse will have to be had to brass-etched sheets applicable to the *Kriegsmarine* as a whole or to other named *Kriegsmarine* ships featuring similar fittings.

The brief reviews which follow are not intended to be exhaustive, and neither is it claimed that all kits and models of pocket battleships are given mention.

Plastic kits

Italeri: *Deutschland* (1/720)

New warship kits from Italeri (formerly known as Aliplast, then Italaerei, and then re-spelt) appear only inter-

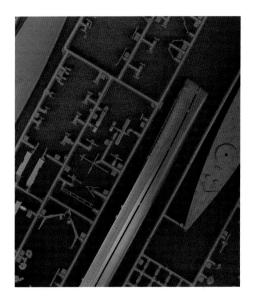

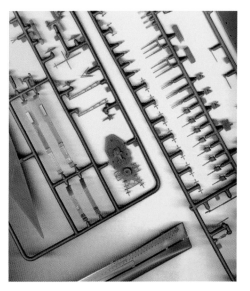

◄◄Parts for Italeri's 1/720 scale kit of *Deutschland*. Notice how the hull halves are moulded in such a way as to facilitate separation for a waterline model if required.

Parts for the Italeri *Admiral Graf Spee*, to the same scale. Both these kits make excellent starting points for accurate miniature replicas.

mittently, and this is something to be regretted from the modeller's point of view because those few released to date have been excellent products. The mouldings are generally sharply defined, the scale effect is very good for injection-moulded kits, and the overall accuracy of the finished models is high. As with all kits from this manufacturer, good eyesight and nimble fingers are called for, since some of the component parts are minuscule in the extreme—bridge instruments, AA mountings etc.

Italeri take a unique line in presenting their hull mouldings, at least as far as these kits are concerned: they are moulded as a single unit, but the above-water and below-water parts are separated by means of small gates which have to be sliced through and cleaned up with abrasive material. Three- or four-way moulds are not used, so the weather decks are separate units, not integral with the hull as in the Japanese Waterline kits. This system saves the modeller the time and trouble involved in sawing away lower hulls if waterline models are required.

The *Deutschland* kit depicts the ship in pre-1938 guise, with flat funnel top and He 60 spotter aircraft (separate floats and propeller!). However, the main turrets are a shade undersize and close-range armament fit is confused: there may well have been ex-

tempore AA fits at the time of the Spanish Civil War, but there appears to be no evidence that, for example, 20mm singles were mounted on the forecastle at that time. The suggested paint scheme is basic, but for those with a steady hand and masking skills can of course be enlivened by the addition of neutrality stripes.

This kit makes up into a convincing little model, and if masts and yards are replaced by finer components it will look even better.

Italeri: *Admiral Graf Spee* (1/720)

The 1970s and 1980s saw the beginnings of some cross-fertilisation amongst the larger kit manufacturers, and this kit was one of the first products to appear under the joint Revell/Italeri label. It is however, an Italeri-engineered kit, distinct in style from the warship kits of the big American manufacturer.

It is, unsurprisingly, the twin of the *Deutschland* kit, sharing a common hull moulding and many components with that product. However, the configuration has been well researched, and the essential characteristics of the most famous of the pocket battleships are accurately conveyed.

→→Components for the 1/700 scale *Deutschland* by Fujimi. Disappointingly, there is no light AA battery amongst them.

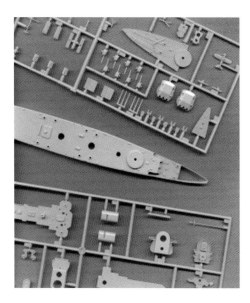

The period depicted is post-1938, with the single searchlight on the forward face of the *Turmmast* and with a representative AA battery (though also with a miniature He 60, not an Ar 196 spotter plane). With little effort—a change of aircraft, the addition of radar etc—and a modification of the suggested overall grey paintwork, a model of the ship as she appeared at the Battle of the River Plate can easily be constructed. Again, the masts, yards and jack and ensign staffs are better replaced by thinner components.

In terms of models from plastic kits, one could not really ask for much more than is provided in the two pocket battleships marketed by Italeri, whose releases are also, at least in the Western Hemisphere, very reasonably priced.

Fujimi: *Deutschland* (1/700)

SEA WAY MODEL　DEUTSCHLAND　FUJIMI

This kit and its sisters from the same company make a very interesting comparison with the two pocket-battleship kits of Italian origin: the sets of mouldings are within a whisker of being to an identical scale. Fujimi is one member of the consortium of Japanese manufacturers who got together in the 1970s to produce the 1/700 scale Waterline Series depict-

ing, initially, Imperial Japanese Navy ships of the Second World War. With the well-known names from the IJN virtually exhausted, the consortium turned its attention to European and American warships, and the pocket battleships were among the early releases.

The hull is a one-piece moulding in keeping with the rest of the kits in the Waterline Series, although the foredeck and the after half of the quarterdeck are separate components. This is not a feature of most of the earlier kits, and requires some explanation because it leaves difficult joints in the model's weather decks which the kit builder has somehow to disguise. Most plastic kit components are produced on a two-way tool—i.e., a 'top' and a 'bottom'—but the hulls in

Deutschland class: Kits and models

	Manufacturer	Scale	Hull	Remarks
Admiral Graf Spee	Clydeside	1/1250	Waterline	Well-detailed wargaming model
Deutschland	Italeri	1/720	Optional	
Admiral Graf Spee	Italeri	1/720	Optional	
Deutschland	Fujimi	1/700	Waterline	
Admiral Graf Spee	Fujimi	1/700	Waterline	
Admiral Scheer	Fujimi	1/700	Waterline	Pre-reconstruction configuration
Admiral Graf Spee	Aurora	1/600	Full hull	Long out of production; collectors' item
Admiral Graf Spee	Airfix	1/600	Full hull	
Admiral Graf Spee	Heller	1/400	Full hull	
Lützow	Heller	1/400	Full hull	
Admiral Scheer	Heller	1/400	Full hull	Post-reconstruction configuration
Admiral Graf Spee	Iron Shipwrights	1/350	Full hull	Resin kit with etched detail parts

the Waterline Series generally utilise four-way tools, which are of course much more complex (and expensive) to design and operate; these enable detail to be reproduced on the 'sides' of plastic kit parts instead of just the 'top' and 'bottom'. The advantages are obvious: difficult hull-to-deck joints are eliminated, while the option of moulding deck fittings and scuttles and hawseholes on the same component is preserved. However, a problem arises where the hull is flared, as it will generally be at the bows. Draw angles for the tools have to be less than 90 degrees in order to achieve release, but this means that flared areas of the hull have to be excessively thick towards the weather decks, and excessively thick plastic components are very vulnerable to shrinkage during cooling, producing the well-known 'sink hole' phenomenon which, if on a visible surface, will look disfiguring. The only certain way that this can be avoided is to arrange for the tool to withdraw from the 'top', where the draw angle can be generous. Modelmakers who

have built early kits from the Waterline Series, with the complete weather deck moulded integrally with the hull, will almost certainly have been faced with irritating sink marks at the bows—often disfiguring the moulded-in hawsers.

This apart, there some other differences of approach between the Japanese and Italian kits. For example, the lower superstructure components in the Fujimi kit are one-piece mouldings and, as a result, the vertical screens lack all but the most basic surface detail; in the Italeri product the screens are separate and fully detailed. The bridge wings in the Fujimi kit have their protective canvas screens moulded *in situ* (and have the appearance of protective plating), whereas the Italeri kit shows simple platforms. There are a host of other minor differences.

As to accuracy, it has to be said that the kit is a little deficient. The period chosen seems to be circa 1939–40, with the new funnel searchlight platform, raked funnel cap (a little understated) and Arado seaplane;

➥ Spread of parts for Fujimi's 1/700 scale *Admiral Scheer*. All three pocket battleships are kitted by this manufacturer as part of the huge Waterline Series.
❚ Two views of the Fujimi *Deutschland*, assembled, painted and detailed by Tony Mollica.

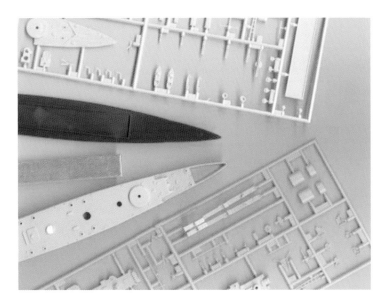

however, there is no light AA battery, which is a glaring omission, and there is no suggestion of any radar equipment. The manufacturers seem to have steered a middle course with regard to bow shape, since it is rather too raked for a pre-reconstruction profile and not raked enough to match the shape following the major repair. The hawsers are moulded in with rubbing plates on the foredeck which the pocket battleships certainly did not possess and the mainmast is incomplete.

On a none-too-distinct profile drawing, the instruction sheet shows a paint scheme with the angled 'dazzle' stripes that the ship wore after her reconstruction, so there is some modification work in store for the kit builder if this scheme is to be applied to an accurate base; the kit's configuration is much more appropriate to 'Weserübung', her first Norwegian deployment.

Fujimi: *Admiral Scheer* (1/700)

Utilising the same hull tools as the foregoing, this kit represents *Scheer* in her pre-1940 state, i.e., prior to reconstruction, but, again, the configuration is a little confused. For example, the

correct-style foremast is there (if set somewhat at a distance from the *Turmmast* structure), but there is a rogue searchlight platform (*à la Spee*) in the front face (which also, to pick nits, has an incorrect arrangement of vision ports) and *Scheer*'s distinctive starboard handling crane immediately abaft and abreast the bridge super-structure—clearly shown in the box-top painting—is ignored in favour of a heavier unit mirroring the port crane abreast the funnel. The funnel cap is flat, but an Arado floatplane is provided: it is not at all clear that *Scheer* embarked an Ar 196 *operationally* prior to the ship's major refit which began in February 1940. The reasons for these hiccoughs become apparent when it is realised that the two moulding frames are identical to those in the *Graf Spee* kit from the same manufacturer, except for a minor modification to one of them so as to include some extra parts for the main-mast structure.

On the credit side, the screens for the forward superstructure (though not those for the after superstructure) are separate from the adjacent deck-ing, enabling detailing to be shown, and, in contrast to the *Deutschland* kit, some light AA gun mouldings are provided.

Fujimi: *Admiral Graf Spee* (1/700)

Like the Italeri offering of the same subject, this kit shows—or purports to show—the ship post-1938 refit, and although from the point of view of accuracy it is the best of the three pocket battleship kits from Fujimi, it is nevertheless not flawless.

Directly comparing the two products, it will be found that the taper of the *Turmmast* in the Italian kit is more pronounced (and more in keep-ing with the real ship, despite the over-scale raised detailing); the foredeck is rather more full (and in fact more accurately portrayed) in the Fujimi kit, which also has the correct shape, in plan view, of the breakwater; Fujimi include an Ar 196 floatplane, though provide only two 20mm mountings (on the funnel platform); and Italeri have the ship's anchors moulded on to the hull while Fujimi furnish them as separate parts. There are other contrasts.

For its kit, Fujimi offer two paint schemes, the prewar overall grey and the camouflage scheme (to a somewhat fanciful pattern, it has to be said) for *Graf Spee*'s wartime career.

Neat, tidy and, by and large, visually accurate, this kit—bearing in mind the points made in the two previous reviews—does justice to a famous subject, and with minor corrective work will certainly look the part.

Airfix: *Admiral Graf Spee* (1/600)

This is one of Airfix's 'mid-term' kits: it is not as aged or basic as the company's *Cossack* or *Victorious*, yet not quite as refined or as sharply tooled as its *Repulse* or *King George V.* It is well designed and has general fidelity, although there a number of features which will require correction if the finished model is to look convincing.

In customary Airfix fashion, the hull is full and comes in port and starboard halves, with the weather decks provided as separate components and having the screens of the superstructure decks moulded on to them. The screens thus have no detail;

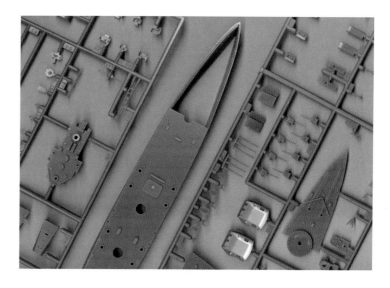

Admiral Graf Spee parts. These assemble into the most accurate of the three 1/700 scale pocket battleships from Fujimi.

Admiral Graf Spee is the most popular of the three pocket battleships as a model subject. This is Fujimi's version, built by Tony Mollica.

↑→ Three views of Alan Chung's model of *Graf Spee* by Fujimi, with guardrail and other detail added.

indeed, with the exception of the hull scuttles and some raised linework on the forward face of the *Turmmast*, the kit is bereft of fine detail in the vertical plane.

Most of the deck fittings are moulded rather than separate features, therein providing the kit modeller with the usual painting challenge (and, as always, one which really must be tackled before the ship's superstructure is built up). An Arado aircraft is provided, and the manufacturers have recognised that the ship was fitted with radar during the period depicted, but there is a scarcity of 20mm weapons.

Three other characteristics of the kit will need to be tackled by the

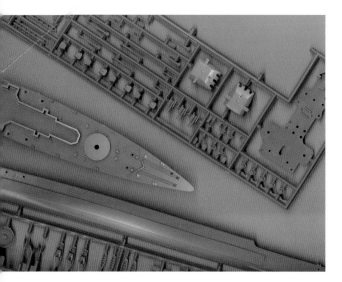
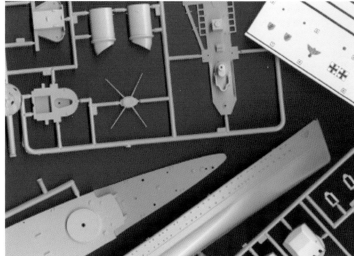

fastidious modeller: the exaggerated 28cm gun barrel jackets will have to be reduced in impact; the odd channels in which the anchor cables are moulded should really be removed (on the actual ship, the cable deck was flush-planked, except for the forepeak); and the stem needs straightening.

Heller: *Lützow* (1/400)

Warship kits from the old-established French company Heller have always evoked interest, in former days because of the manufacturer's single-minded concentration on vessels of the French Navy—though this has softened in recent years—and also because of its adherence to 1/400, which is still its preferred scale despite the choices made by rival companies. All three pocket battleships are represented in the Heller catalogue.

The choice of *Lützow* rather than *Deutschland* indicates a welcome spirit of adventure on the part of the manufacturer, since kits showing the ship later in her career are not common. The date chosen is not indicated, but it is post-reconstruction of course,

with the final shape of the funnel cap evident, dating it as 1942 or later. However, since the medium and light flak armament is limited to two 3.7cm twins and four 20mm singles, and because only one radar aerial is displayed at the foretop, it is difficult to say what state has been selected. The overall grey colour scheme suggests Norway in mid-1942.

The general layout of the kit is good, and the little Arado seaplane and the ship's boats are neat affairs (Heller have always been good at ship's boats). The tubular foremast is too slim, however, and there is rather too much angle to the faces of the main turrets. The little alterations that are necessary can all be accommodated; much more of a problem is the shape of the bows, which are too short, show a stem raked rather aggressively and, most seriously of all, have far too little flare, resulting in a foredeck which is much too slim and pointed.

Heller: *Admiral Scheer* (1/400)

This differs from the *Lützow* kit in having a totally new pair of hull mouldings—the finished model is in

↑ Parts for the Airfix kit of *Admiral Graf Spee* in 1/600 scale.
↑ Heller offer all three pocket battleships in their standard 1/400 scale, two of them in post-reconstruction configuration. These are some of the parts for *Lützow*.

early post-reconstruction configuration—and two out of three moulding frames changed to incorporate parts applicable to *Scheer*; the ship's boats, gun mountings, torpedo tube racks, spotter plane, etc are identical to those in the other two kits in the series. It also has a weather deck split amidships into two halves. This time Heller have captured the bow form rather better: the curve of the stem is about right, and the foredeck better proportioned if still perhaps a touch sharp. The fastidious will wish to relocate the 15cm gun positions: the forward pair on either side are rather too far forward and the after pair too far aft; furthermore, the spacing between the after pair on either side is too great, the arrangement being quite symmetrical which Heller's is not—a flaw evident in all three kits of the class.

For the rest, the kit is to the usual Heller standard—good basic material which with thinning, shaping and detailing to taste, can result in a fine model. The standard inclusions with ship kits from this manufacurer—neat metallic anchor cable, and extremely sturdy injection-moulded guard rail—are there of course.

The instruction sheet suggests an all-grey finish rather than the camouflage scheme the ship wore during her sojourn in Norwegian waters, while a neat decal sheet is of limited value in that it furnishes the bow shield sported by the ship prior to her reconstruction and a *Reich* battle ensign from

which, as usual, the Nazi emblem has been excised.

Heller: *Admiral Graf Spee* (1/400)

This has much the same ingredients as the two previous kits, but this time with an almost perfect bow and foredeck shape, making the hull well worth utilising if the modelmaker is considering building miniature replicas of *Deutschland* and *Scheer* in early guise. Setting aside the general comments made earlier, the fidelity of this kit is good, and a convincing model will result with minimal modification. *Graf Spee* was, of course, little altered during her short career, so a pre-war or wartime finish is easily depicted, and those requiring something a little different can reproduce in miniature the *Graf Spee*'s crewmen's work and fabricate a dummy after funnel and third main turret.

This is probably the best of the three Heller 1/400 scale pocket battleships.

Accessory Packs

The manufacture of 'after-market' accessories for modelmakers continues to

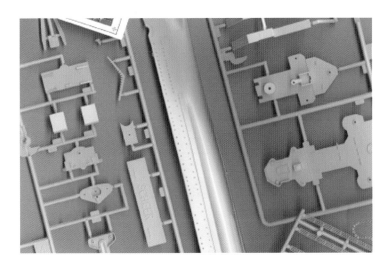

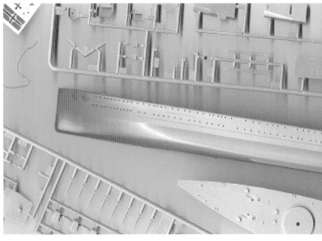

be a growth industry, and while, at the time of writing, there is relatively little available pertaining directly to pocket battleships, there is a good range of etched-metal frets covering the *Kriegsmarine* as a whole; for those requiring a little extra, the *Scharnhorst* class battleships and *Admiral Hipper* class cruisers are given extensive treatment by one of the manufacturers, and much of the metalwork included on these is applicable also to the *Deutschland* class.

It must be appreciated that such etched items as deck rail—even that provided in the class-specific sets—is unavoidably arbitrary in nature, and will generally be used by the modelmaker for effect only. The brass rail provided by the specialist manufacturers is 'regular' in concept: distances between stanchions vary, especially around smaller platforms and curved decking, and, moreover, different manufacturers have a different spacing policy. A good deal of compromise

---

German Pocket Battleships: Accessories

At the time of writing, it is believed that there are no accessory sets produced specifically for models of the pocket battleships. The list below therefore gives an indication of the more general sets relevant to the three ships.

Manufacturer	Scale	Remarks
Eduard	1/700	*Kriegsmarine* deck rail
Eduard	1/700	*Scharnhorst* fittings
White Ensign Models	1/700	*Kriegsmarine* Generic Fittings
White Ensign Models	1/700	WW2 German AA Weapons
White Ensign Models	1/700	Ladders and Walkways
Gold Medal Models	1/700	German Warship Fittings
White Ensign Models	1/600	*Kriegsmarine* Generic Fittings
White Ensign Models	1/600	WW2 German AA Weapons
Gold Medal Models	1/600	German Warship Fittings
Eduard	1/450	*Kriegsmarine* deck rail
White Ensign Models	1/400	*Scharnhorst* and *Gneisenau*
White Ensign Models	1/400	*Prinz Eugen* and *Admiral Hipper*
Gold Medal Models	1/400	German Warship Fittings
Eduard	1/350	*Bismarck* fittings
Eduard	1/350	*Kriegsmarine* deck rail

In addition to above, WEM and GMM produce deck rail, ladders, walkways etc in 1/700, 1/600, 1/400 and 1/350 scales; and L'Arsénal manufactures 20mm weapons and deck rail in 1/400 scale. GMM and Dunagain also issue general decal sheets in 1/700 and 1/350 scale containing such items as flags and pennants, while GMM produces 1/700 and 1/350 scale naval figures, WEM 1/350 scale naval figures and Tom's Modelworks 1/600 scale figures.

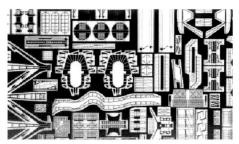

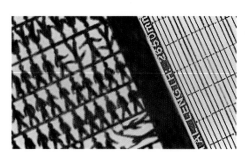

will be required on the part of the modelmaker who uses proprietory deck rail in order to ensure that fairleads, bollards, etc are cleared correctly; except in extremely rare instances where fully comprehensive photographic coverage of a subject vessel may be available, a good deal of guesswork will have to be employed when fitting the rail around the more inaccessible platforms; and even the finest etched deck rail will be a little overscale—the more so when a coat of paint is applied. The other point is that, ignoring the gauge of the brass, etched frets are two-dimensional ('flat'), unlike the real thing. But there is a limit to what can be achieved, even in larger scales: all is a compromise!

Acknowledgement

Acknowledgement is made of the following companies, who kindly provided samples for the purposes of these reviews: Heller SA, White Ensign Models, Tom's Modelworks.

◄◄Gold Medal Models' 1/700 scale German warship fittings.

◄◄White Ensign Models' *Kriegsmarine* fittings—one of three 'Ultimate' sets available from this manufacturer in 1/600 scale.

◄◄Tom's Modelworks' 1/600 scale naval figures and Eduard's 1/700 scale *Kriegsmarine* guardrail..

Modelmakers' Showcase

↓ Two views of Heller's *Graf Spee*, constructed by Michael A. Taylor of Taylor Made Miniatures—as a diversion from his more serious work! The photo-etch details are from Gold Medal Models.

WHAT is a model for? Why create a replica-in-miniature of anything? It depends. Some modellers argue that the creation of a model gives them an insight into a piece of engineering and therefore is educative; or perhaps the research involved in the production of a model is the primary concern. Others will say that the creation of a model provides a relaxing pastime, enabling them to forget the stresses and strains of everyday life. Others see model-making as a means to an end: their real hobby is wargaming, and models enable them to re-enact pieces of history; or perhaps the main interest is sailing model boats and ships, and the model is the tool which enables them to indulge in their hobby.

Whatever the motivation, the pursuit of excellence is, by and large, the common theme amongst model-makers. Plastic kits provide a short-cut to the objective; building a plastic model and modifying and detailing it to make it appear more realistic is a further stage; and models created entirely from scratch, using basic reference tools, is a third approach. All three interests are evident in the following pages, but the end result is the same—an object to admire.

↓ The large-scale model of *Admiral Scheer* on display at the National Maritime Museum in Greenwich, London.

ADMIRAL GRAF SPEE 1/100 scale Peter Behmüller

There is a tendency for modelmakers to fall into one of two categories: the 'static' modeller, whose interest lies in the pursuit of accuracy and minute detail, and the model boat enthusiast, whose joy is to create a working model (preferably a really large one) which can be put through its paces at the local lake. The one cannot withstand rough handling; the other has to cope with the rigours of regular transportation, wind and weather, and the occasional damaging blow. Rare indeed is the modelmaker who succeeds in combining the two interests, but Peter Behmüller is one, and his working model of *Graf Spee* stands comparison with the best of the static models.

Peter Behmüller's 1/100 scale model of *Admiral Graf Spee* utilises kit parts for the hull and the 15cm, 3.7cm and 2cm armament but the remainder is scratchbuilt. The main propulsion system is powered by two 12V batteries and the model has a sailing endurance of over three hours.

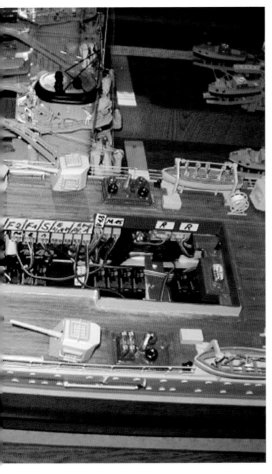

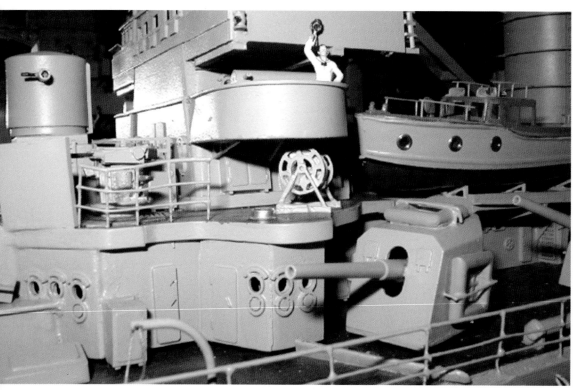

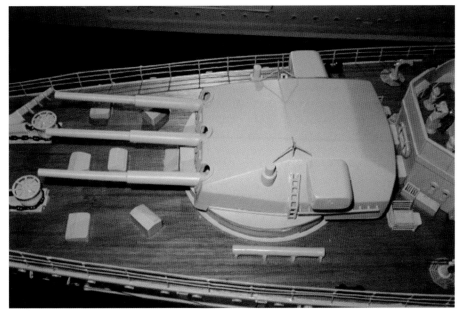

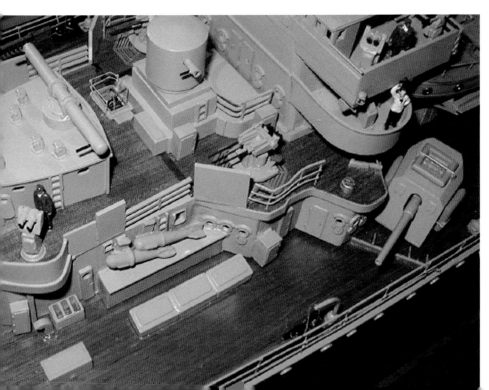

In addition to its main propulsion drive, the model features over 30 'extras', including main turret rotation and gun elevation; secondary turret rotation; an onboard smoke generator discharging through the funnel; a foghorn; and a sound system which plays martial music. The model is finished in RAL 7001/FS36620 grey, with the underwater hull in red oxide (RAL 3009). The deck is teak planked. Plans from Vth Verlag in Baden-Baden were used as the main reference source, with additional details checked from photographs etc.

ADMIRAL GRAF SPEE   1/350 scale   Dave Judy

Dave Judy's model of *Admiral Graf Spee* is built from the Iron Shipwrights kit, which comprises resin components for the major structures, white metal for smaller parts, brass rod for masts etc, brass chain for the anchor cables and etched brass for fine details such as guardrail.

Although their labour-intensive production processes and short mould life makes them relatively expensive to produce, resin kits have increased in popularity enormously over recent years, and the level of detail achievable in resin castings can surpass that of the best injection-moulded kits. Careful preparation of the parts is essential, filling any voids that may have been produced by air bubbles in the casting process and sanding off 'pour plugs'. Gluing is best carried out using cyanoacrylate glue ('superglue'), and cleaning the parts thoroughly prior to painting them is required because of release agents and the amount of dust created during preparation.

◄ Dave Judy's completed model of the Iron Shipwrights *Admiral Graf Spee*, presented here on a custom-built base, is a good example of the high standards that can be achieved using resin kits. Low production runs and labour-intensive tooling inevitably results in high retail prices: this kit currently (2002) sells for about $240–250 (£150–160); a comparable injection-moulded kit might cost $30–40 (£20–25) plus 'after market' accessories.

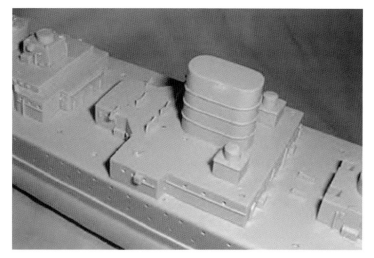

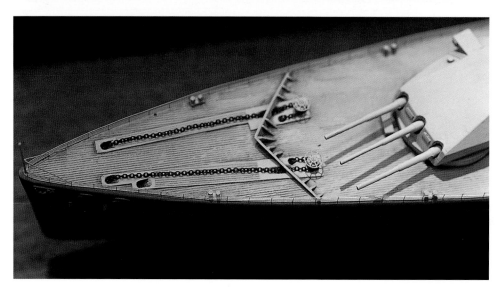

Dave Judy's model is built with little modification: the kit contains everything needed to produce a finely detailed showpiece. Assembling a resin kit calls for vigilance and patience because procedures are slower and more intricate than with injection-moulded kits, one reason being the need to shape parts where the pour plugs—equivalent to moulding gates in plastic kits—are present.

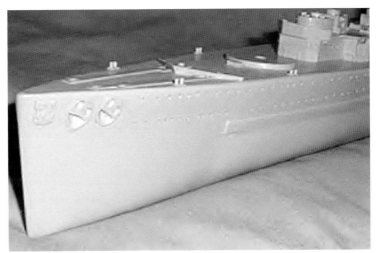

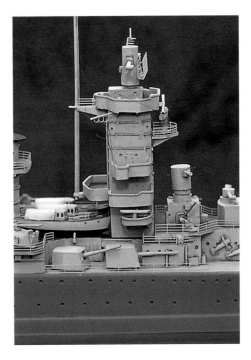

Schemes

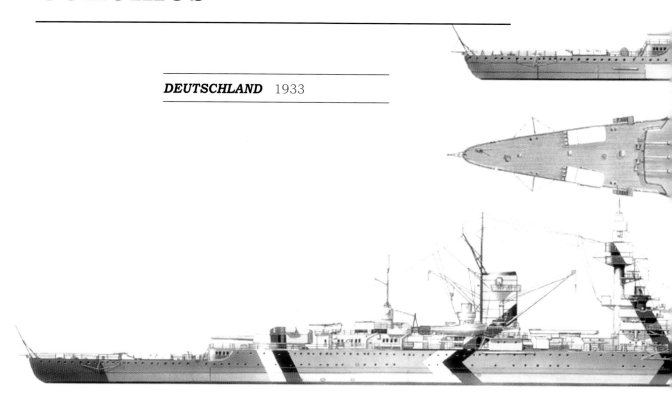

DEUTSCHLAND 1933

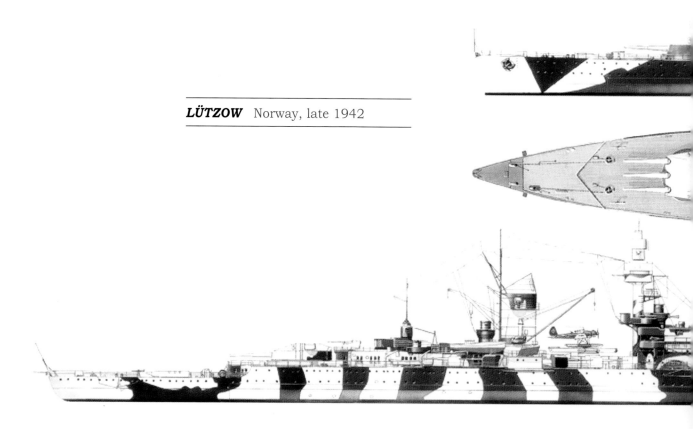

LÜTZOW Norway, late 1942

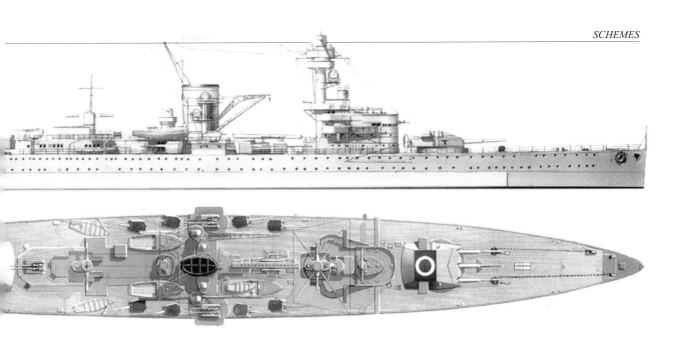

LÜTZOW Baltic, 1941

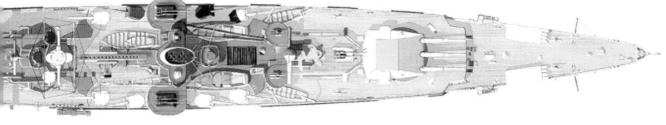

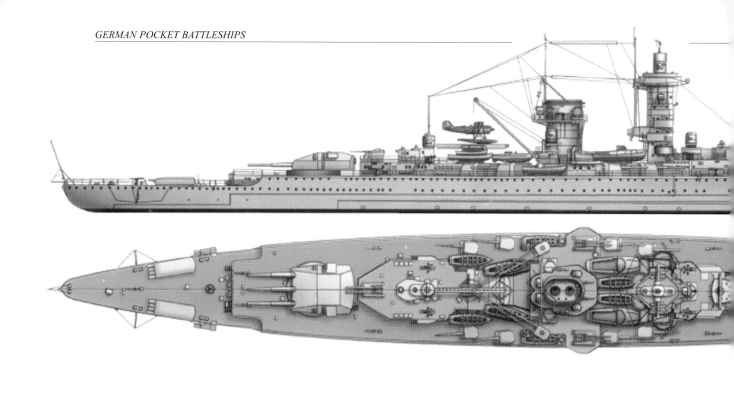

ADMIRAL SCHEER 1940

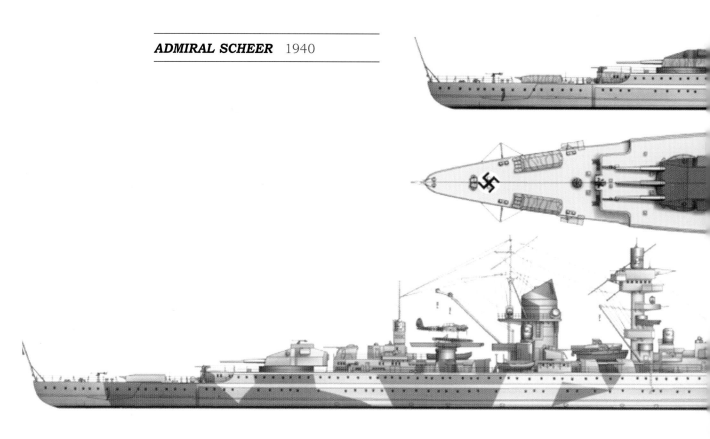

ADMIRAL SCHEER 1943

ADMIRAL SCHEER 1939

Bow shield, 1937–40

Skagerrak Skagerrak

Port   Starboard

ADMIRAL SCHEER 1942

ADMIRAL GRAF SPEE 1938

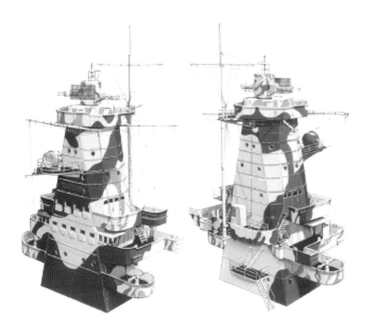

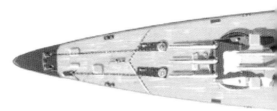

Scrap views showing camouflage pattern on *Turmmast*

Heinkel He 60 floatplane
operated by *Admiral
Scheer* 1938

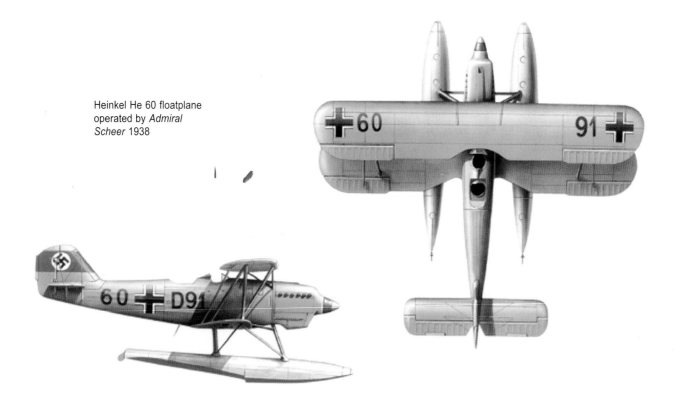

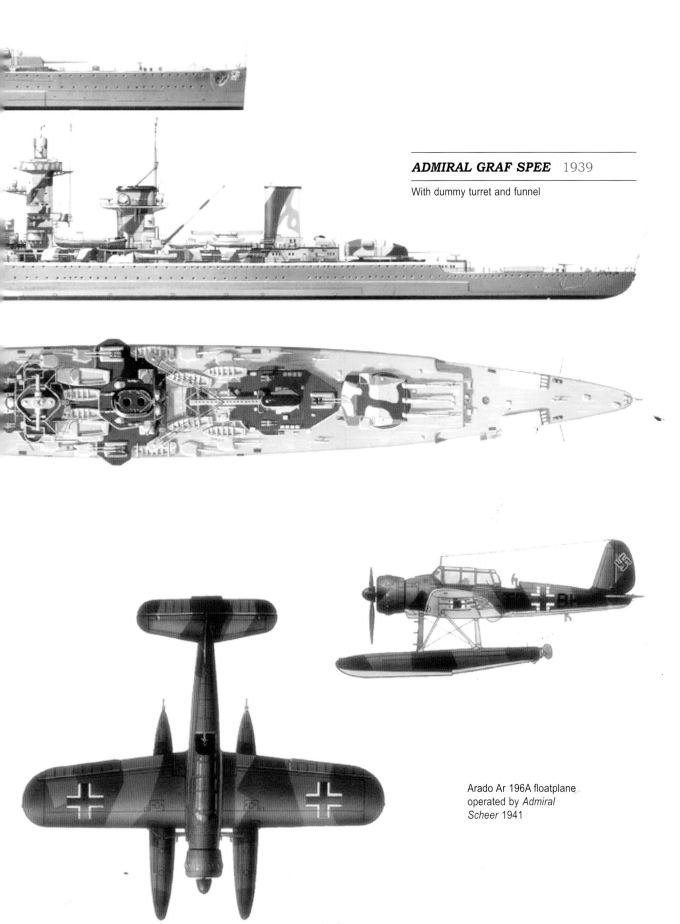

ADMIRAL GRAF SPEE 1939

With dummy turret and funnel

Arado Ar 196A floatplane
operated by *Admiral
Scheer* 1941

43

ADMIRAL GRAF SPEE 1/100 scale Neptune Ship Modelling Club

Based in Makeyevka, in the Ukraine, the Neptune Ship Modelling Club is an unusual association encompassing both professional and amateur model-makers. Its work has evolved from modelling for fun and relaxation into the commercial production of highly detailed, large-scale models of ships of all eras for individual clients.

▮ The 1/100 scale model of *Admiral Graf Spee*, a collective building project undertaken by the members of the Neptune Club. The model is approximately 6ft 1½in (187cm) long. Note that the heraldic device on the bow has yet to be added.

← The superstructure, main turrets and 10.5cm mountings are detachable. Various metals, plastics and leaf brass were used in the manufacture of these components.

→ A close-in view of the funnel, catapult and ship's boats, showing the superb craftsmanship which has been applied to this model, Note, in particular, the carefully prepared guardrail, the intricate davits, the funnel cap detail and the realistic search-lights. The Arado 196 even has a pilot!

→→ More skilled work-manship is evident around the *Turmmast*: note, amongst a pleth-ora of fine detail, the neatly executed con-tours of the protective plating. The model represents the ship post-1938, with the new searchlight plat-form facing forward.

↓ An overall view of the Neptune Club's *Admiral Graf Spee* in 1/100 scale. The hull is a fibreglass moulding, and turrets and directors are rotatable. The model occupied the members of the club for two years, and it won silver medals at the Ukraine Championships in 1998 and 1999.

←Foredeck detail, showing some of the carefully produced deck fittings and anchor cable. All the weather decks on the model are made from natural wood.

⬆ Close in to the after superstructure and 28cm turret, offering a view of the anti-aircraft armament, the awning stanchions, main turret detailing and companion ladder. The realistic planking shows up well in this photograph.

Ship's Aircraft

1:200 scale

HEINKEL He 60

Span 42ft 4½.in (13.5m); length 37ft 8˚in (11.5m); height 16ft 2˚in (5.3m). One BMW VI 6.0 ZU 12-cyl liquid-cooled engine (660hp). Speed 140mph max, 118mph cruise. Range 478 miles max.

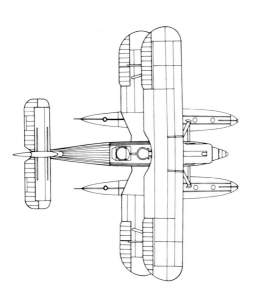

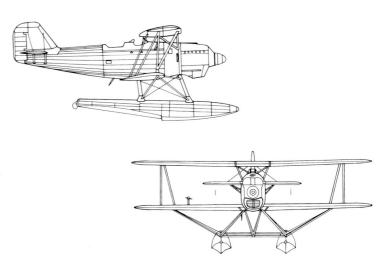

ARADO Ar196

Span 40ft 9˚in (12.4m); length 35ft 11˚in (10.2m); height 14ft 7in (5.0m). One BMW 132K 9-cyl radial air-cooled engine (960hp). Speed 194mph max, 166mph cruise. Range 497 miles max.

1:200 scale

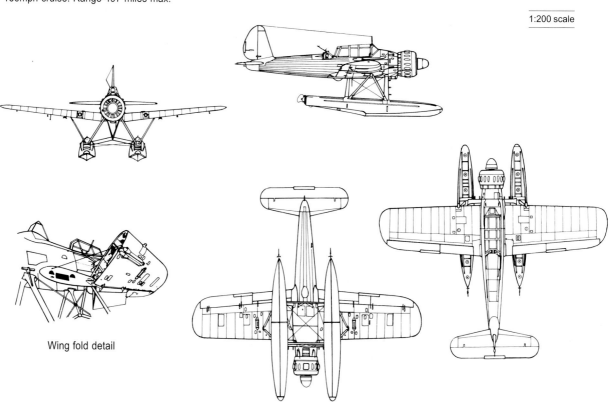

Wing fold detail

Appearance

ALTHOUGH these three ships were built to a common design, there were, as noted earlier, significant differences in appearance, even as built. *Admiral Graf Spee*, the last of the trio to be completed, was an early war loss and did not undergo major modification during her service, but both *Deutschland* (*Lützow*) and *Admiral Scheer*, in addition to receiving periodic upgrades, were substantially reconstructed during the war.

DEUTSCHLAND (*LÜTZOW*)

When she commissioned on 1 April 1933, *Deutschland* was hardly the finished article. She had no aircraft catapult, neither her 3.7cm nor her 2cm AA weapons (nor the associated fire control facilities) were installed, she shipped ancient 8.8cm heavy AA guns in single mountings and her torpedo tubes were of an interim design. Thus her first 'refit', in 1934–35, was in effect a completion of the fitting-out process, bringing her equipment into line with the specifications of the final design.

After her stern was wrecked by the British submarine *Spearfish* on 11 April 1940, the opportunity was taken to modify the bows, and *Lützow* (as *Deutschland* was now renamed) emerged 1.9m longer and with a raked stem. (The extremely pronounced flare just beneath the weatherdeck gives the impression in some photographs that

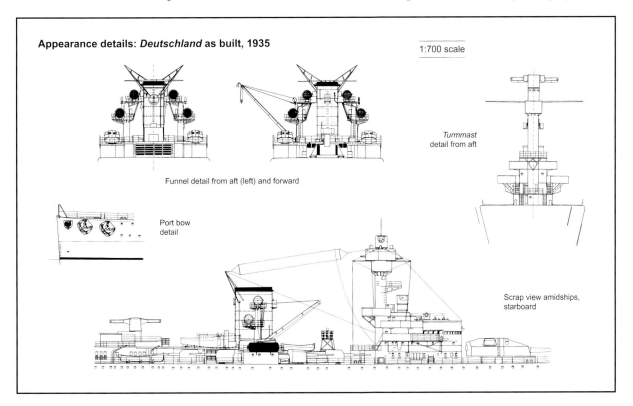

Appearance details: *Deutschland* as built, 1935

1:700 scale

Funnel detail from aft (left) and forward

Turmmast detail from aft

Port bow detail

Scrap view amidships, starboard

Refit Summary: *Deutschland/Lützow*

Dates	Location	Details
Dec 1934–Feb 1935	Wilhelmshaven	Platform added to foretop; after main rangefinder modified; port derrick replaced by crane; mainmast added to funnel; 3 x 1 8.8cm replaced by 3 x 2 8.8cm; 4 x 2 3.7cm, 6 x 2 2cm added; SL 2 AA fire control added; 50cm torpedo tubes replaced by 53.3cm; catapult added and aircraft embarked
1937	Wilhelmshaven	Derrick and crane renewed; FuMG 39 radar added
Early 1938	Wilhelmshaven	Raked funnel cap added
Summer 1939	Wilhelmshaven	FuMG 39 radar replaced by FuMO 22; He 60 aircraft replaced by Ar 196
Aug–Dec 1940	Kiel	Hull lengthened by 2m to incorporate semi-clipper bow and after port main hawser deleted; stern repaired; 3 x 2 8.8cm replaced by 3 x 10.5cm; numerous 2cm added
Aug-Oct 1942	Kiel	FuMO 22 radar replaced by 2 x FuMO 26, FuMB 4 added; funnel cap renewed
Nov 1943–Feb 1944	Libau	1 x FuMO 26 deleted; 6 x 1 4cm added and 2cm weapons increased to 3 x 4, 6 x 2 and 2 x 1
Early 1945		Short-range AA armament increased to ten 3.7cm and twenty-eight 2cm

the bow was of 'clipper' shape, but this was not the case.) Prewar Atlantic voyages had demonstrated that the pocket-battleships were not particularly good sea boats, being very wet forward and aft and having poor rolling qualities—the former problem afflicting the battleships *Scharnhorst* and *Gneisenau* as well. Plans to recon-

struct the class were drawn up well before the Second World War broke out, but were put into effect only in 1940—and then only in a limited way (for example, the drastic step of widening the beam was quickly abandoned when hostilities began). Interference from funnel smoke was also a constant problem: a gently raked funnel cap

➡ Views of *Deutschland* (clockwise from top left): fitting out 'Anton' turret, 1932; fitting out the foward superstructure, 1932; amidships from starboard, 1936; and port Nos 1 and 2 15cm turrets, with the port 8.8cm beyond, 1937.

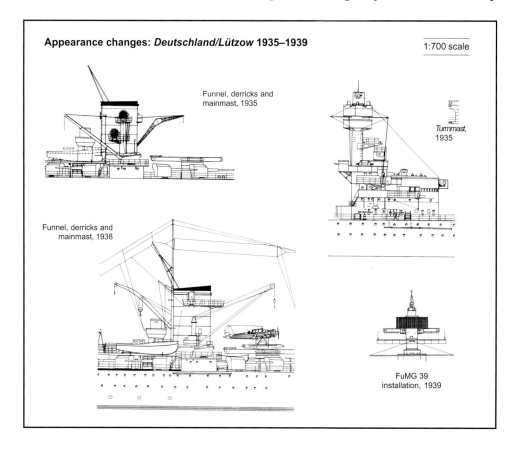

Appearance changes: *Deutschland/Lützow* 1935–1939

1:700 scale

Funnel, derricks and mainmast, 1935

Turmmast, 1935

Funnel, derricks and mainmast, 1938

FuMG 39 installation, 1939

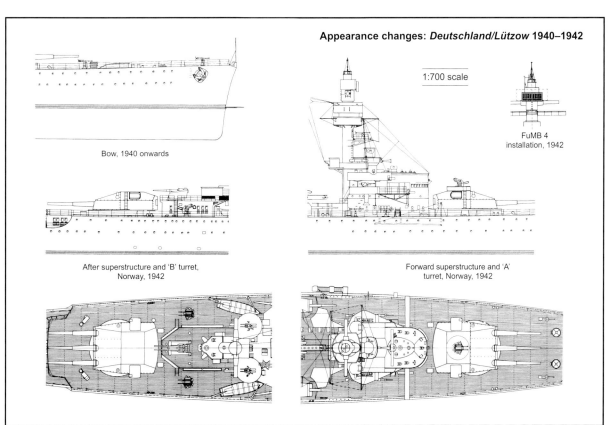

Appearance changes: *Deutschland/Lützow* 1940–1942

1:700 scale

FuMB 4
installation, 1942

Bow, 1940 onwards

After superstructure and 'B' turret,
Norway, 1942

Forward superstructure and 'A'
turret, Norway, 1942

Deutschland with a coating of frost on 'A' turret during a North European winter, and with Spanish Civil War neutrality stripes prominent.

was added in 1938, but it proved to be inadequate to the task and a much taller and more sharply raked cap was introduced in the 1942 refit.

In common with all major warships, the anti-aircraft battery was progressively strengthened as the conflict wore on and the incidence of aerial attack became more frequent and weapon-aiming more accurate. A good deal of maintenance and modification were also necessary with regard to the *Panzerschiffe* diesel machinery, although the impact of this work on the vessel's external appearance was minimal.

Prior to 1939 the ship was painted in *Kriegsmarine* light grey overall; most pre-war and early-war broadside photographs of pocket-battleships give the impression that the hull may have been painted in a distinctly darker shade of grey than the upperworks, but this is a trick of the light produced by the marked flare of the ships' hulls throughout their length. However, from a very early date (certainly from 1934 onwards) the horizontal surfaces of *Deutschland*'s main and secondary gun houses were finished in dark grey, that on 'A' turret having in addition a 1m wide circular band painted in white as an aerial recognition symbol. The principal weather decks, with the ex-

ception of the tip of the forecastle, were left in natural wood, and the superstructure platforms were probably finished in the same grey as the vertical surfaces. From 1936 until 1938—during the time of the Spanish Civil War—both main turrets sported three athwartships stripes, approximately 1m wide, in the national colours of red,

Deutschland's *Turmmast*, showing the 10.5cm range-finder at the foretop, the searchlight platform beneath the gunnery control platform and, to the port side, one of the SL 2 AA directors.

Lützow in disruptive camouflage, probably late 1942 or early 1943, and with FuMB 4 *Samos* and FuMO 26 radar antennas at the foretop.

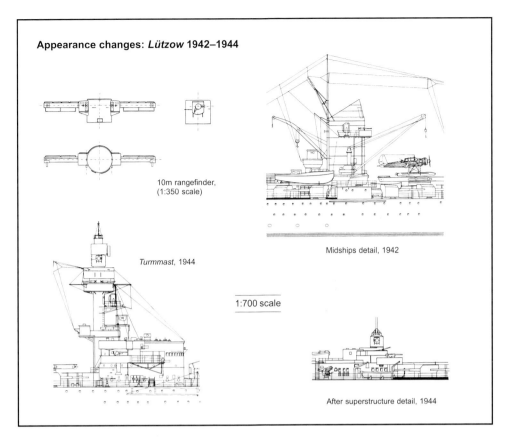

Appearance changes: *Lützow* 1942–1944

10m rangefinder, (1:350 scale)

Turmmast, 1944

1:700 scale

Midships detail, 1942

After superstructure detail, 1944

white and back, black towards amidships in each instance.

The ship continued in this general scheme until 1941, when, in March or April, she had black and white 'dazzle' bands applied to hull and superstructure and dark grey to the stem and stern—the so-called 'Baltic

camouflage scheme' in vogue at that time. After the refit of 1942 she wore an overall dark grey, but while in Norwegian waters in 1942 she was painted up in disruptive camouflage: the striking contrast between the two colours suggest that the latter were dark and light grey. It is unclear how long this scheme was in place: it was apparently still evident during 1943, but by 1944 there had been a return to overall grey. Information concerning colours for this last year of the war is sketchy, but it would appear that light grey paintwork was carried for a period, while during the final months a return to a much darker hue was made.

ADMIRAL SCHEER

Although *Admiral Scheer* was the sister-ship of the earlier *Deutschland*, she was by no means an identical copy. Most obviously, the tubular foremast/bridge structure was aban-

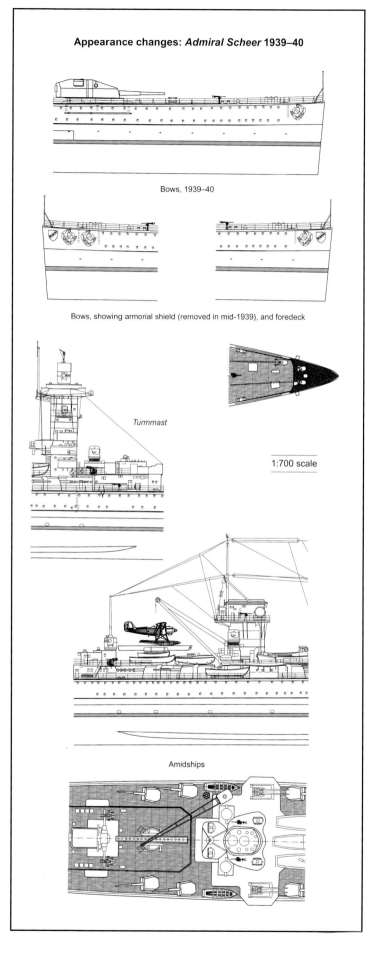

Appearance changes: *Admiral Scheer* **1939–40**

Bows, 1939–40

Bows, showing armorial shield (removed in mid-1939), and foredeck

Turmmast

1:700 scale

Amidships

←← ↓*Admiral Scheer*, port side amidships, with a pinnace being hoisted.
↑ ←One of *Scheer*'s 15cm turrets, showing frontal detail.
↑ ➞ Forepeak, about 1935, showing armorial shield.

doned in favour of a more substantial, tapering tower (although ironically, with topweight a serious problem, *Scheer* reverted to a tubular structure later in her career). More subtly, *Scheer* was almost 1m beamier than *Deutschland*, had an anti-roll stabilisation system fitted (it was later discarded), and had a slightly different armour scheme; moreover, her *Turm-* *mast* was sited some 2.5m further aft, and her funnel about 1.5m further forward, than her classmate's; and, as a result, the aircraft catapult and stowage facilities were sited abaft rather than forward of the funnel.

Scheer underwent a major refit in the first half of 1940. The hull was lengthened in the same manner as would *Deutschland*'s later that year,

Refit Summary: *Admiral Scheer*

Dates	Location	Details
1935–1936		Catapult and aircraft handling crane added and aircraft embarked
Oct 1937	Wilhelmshaven	Admiral's bridge added to forward superstructure; gaffs added to foretop and mainmast
1939	Wilhelmshaven	Handling crane abreast funnel replaced; FuMO 22 cupola added to foretop; He 60 spotter aircraft replaced by Ar 196
1 Feb-31 July 1940	Wilhelmshaven	*Turmmast* removed and replaced by tubular bridge structure; bows lengthened by 1.9m and remodelled to incorporate raked stem; hawseholes repositioned; new raked funnel cap added and funnel platform enlarged; new mainmast fitted; 3 x 3 8.8cm heavy AA replaced by 3 x 2 10.5cm; light AA augmented; handling crane renewed
1941		FuMO 26 radar added to after control platform
Dec 1942–mid 1943	Wilhelmshaven/ Swinemünde	Bridge and foretop modified; raked cap added to funnel and one searchlight deleted from funnel platform; FuMO 22 replaced by FuMO 26 (2 aerials); 1 x Timor and 4 x Sumatra aerials added
1944	Gotenhafen	1 x FuMO 26 deleted; close-range AA increased to 6 x 1 4cm, 2 x 2 3.7cm and 3 x 4, 6 x 2 and 2 x 1 2cm
1945		2 x 2 3.7cm, seven (7 x 1?) 20mm added

Plans

ADMIRAL GRAF SPEE 1939

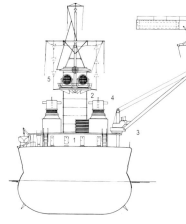

1:700 scale

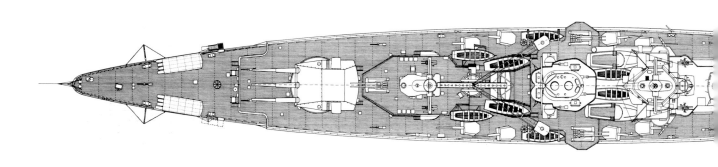

Station 28°

Station 36

Station 58°

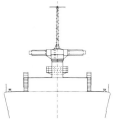

Station 67

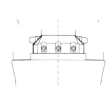

Station 45

Station 89

Station 75

Station 89

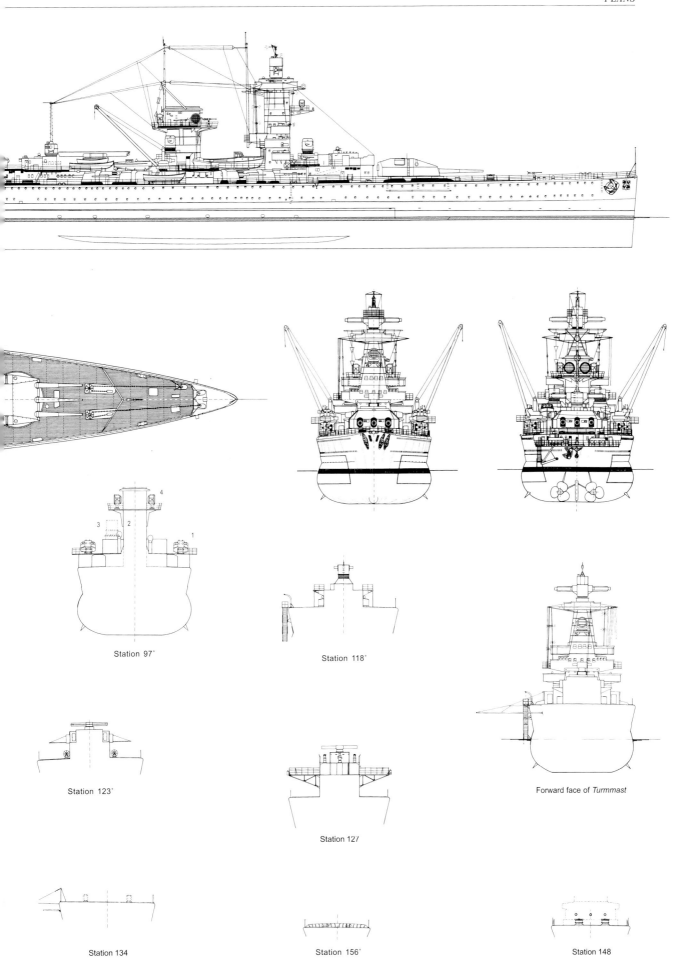

Station 97˚

Station 118˚

Station 123˚

Station 127

Forward face of *Turmmast*

Station 134

Station 156˚

Station 148

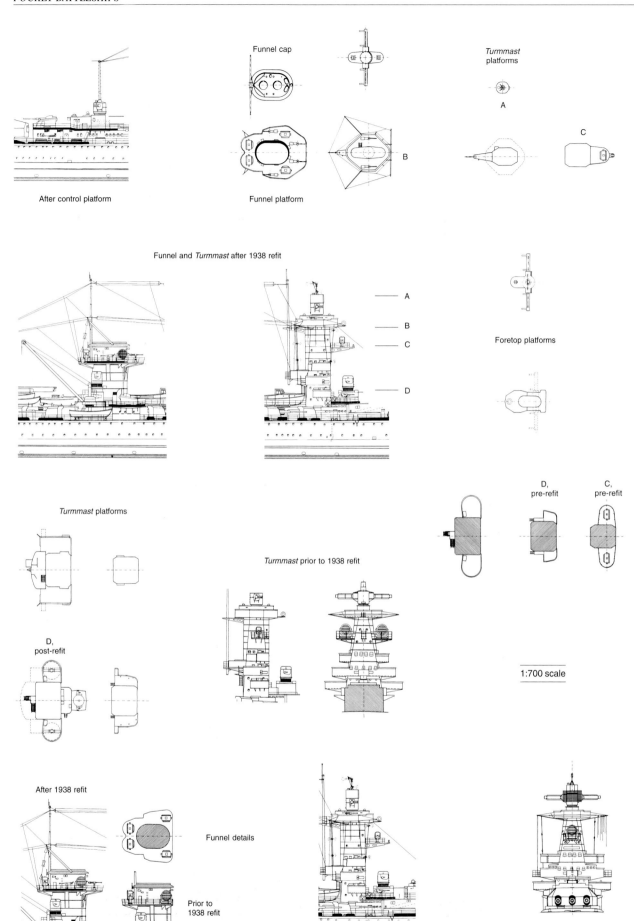

After control platform

Funnel cap

Funnel platform

Turmmast platforms

A

C

B

Funnel and *Turmmast* after 1938 refit

A

B

C

D

Foretop platforms

D, pre-refit

C, pre-refit

Turmmast platforms

Turmmast prior to 1938 refit

D, post-refit

1:700 scale

After 1938 refit

Funnel details

Prior to 1938 refit

Turmmast after 1938 refit

ADMIRAL GRAF SPEE 1939 (continued)

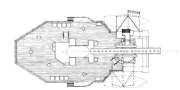

After shelter deck, showing
aircraft catapult

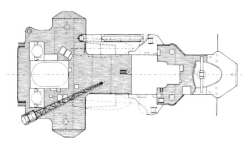

Forward shelter deck

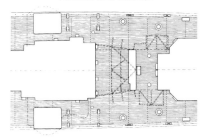

Forecastle deck, amidships

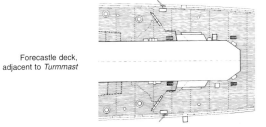

Forecastle deck,
adjacent to *Turmmast*

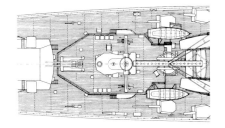

After shelter deck, showing AA
armament layout

Details of aircraft landing
mat (this was jettisoned
during the 1939 South
Atlantic raiding cruise)

Bow, port side, showing anchor
and shield details

Amidships profile,
after 1938 refit

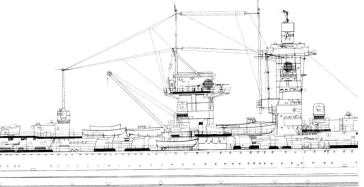

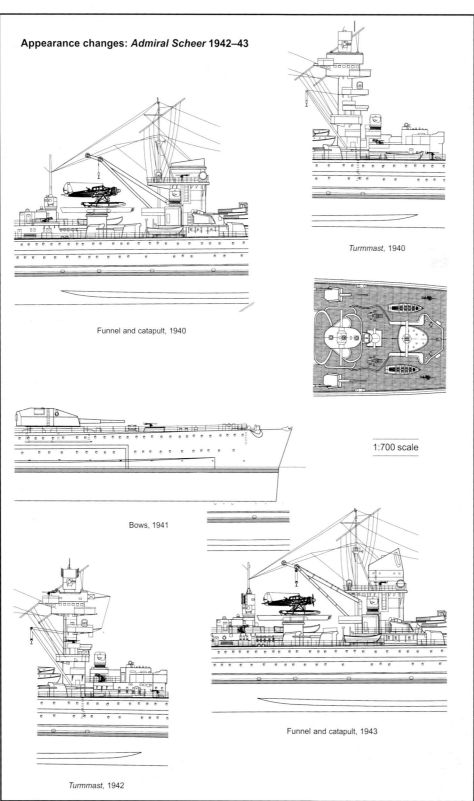

Appearance changes: *Admiral Scheer* **1942–43**

Funnel and catapult, 1940

Turmmast, 1940

1:700 scale

Bows, 1941

Funnel and catapult, 1943

Turmmast, 1942

↑ New bow, new *Turmmast*, new funnel cap and new main-mast—the four striking outward modifications following *Admiral Scheer*'s reconstruc-tion in 1940.

and also incorporated a raked stem, but the new forward superstructure, though essentially a tubular *Turm-mast*, was of a quite different configuration from that which was a feature of *Deutschland* from the start.

As the war ground on, additional anti-aircraft guns were installed aboard, and radar was upgraded.

Scheer wore four distinct paint schemes during the course of her career. From the time of commissioning until the outbreak of war she was finished in the standard *Kriegs-marine* light grey with dark grey turret tops as in her sister-ship, relieved during the time of the Spanish Civil War by neutrality bands around the main turrets. Following her major refit in 1940, she retained the standard grey hull, but her upperworks were dappled in camouflage paint (probably olive green) and her main turret tops were painted red. In 1942, for her service in Norway, she was repainted with angular areas of dark grey over all vertical surfaces in an attempt to break up the outline of the ship. (It would appear that this scheme was re-applied at least once, the second time with a different pattern.) Finally, during her last months in the Baltic, she reverted to overall grey.

ADMIRAL GRAF SPEE

The last ship of the class to be completed also had the shortest career, surviving the outbreak of war by only 3° months, though not before she had managed to wreak some havoc in the shipping lanes of the Atlantic and Indian Oceans.

Refit Summary: *Admiral Graf Spee*		
Date	Location	Details
Sep–Oct 1938		Modifications to foretop and searchlight platforms on *Turmmast*; 6 x 2 88cm replaced by 6 x 10.5cm; FuMO 22 radar system added

↑ A prewar view of *Graf Spee*'s forward super-structure. The legend on the face of the *Turm-mast*—'Coronel'—commemorates *Vizeadmiral* Maximilian *Graf* von Spee's victory over the British cruisers *Good Hope* and *Monmouth* in November 1914 off the coast of Chile.
↑➡ Close-in view of the *Turmmast*, port side, after the River Plate engagement. The hole below the foretop platform was made by an 8in shell from *Exeter*.

In configuration, *Graf Spee* closely resembled *Scheer* but, again, differed in detail. She had a pagoda-like *Turm-mast* very similar to that installed aboard *Scheer*, but the arrangement of the platforms and the location of the foremast were distinguishing features, as was the design of the funnel plat-form. During her one and only raiding cruise an attempt to disguise the appearance of the ship was made by crew members, a second 'funnel' and a superfiring 'turret' forward of the bridge being fashioned from wood and

canvas, though these subterfuges had been discarded by the time of the River Plate action.

For her Spanish Civil War deployments, *Graf Spee* retained the standard grey finish, with neutrality bands in red, white and black athwartships across the main turrets; these were applied in the same way those painted on her sister-ships, although for one deployment at least they took the form of two sets of stripes (with black furthest from the centre in each case) either side of the rangefinder. Some time before 21 August 1939 she had disruptive camouflage applied to her upperworks, with large irregular bands of dark grey interspersed with a smaller-scale pattern of either medium grey or medium green (the matter is contentious), and fake bow and secondary waves were applied in white to the hull. This scheme was maintained until the ship's loss.

↑ *Graf Spee* during her raiding cruise, showing the fake after funnel and fake main turret rigged to deceive.

↓ A battle-scarred *Graf Spee* at Montevideo. Temporary repairs have been effected.

Selected References

BOOKS

Beisheim, Peter (ed.), *Building Model Warships of the Iron and Steel Eras*, Chatham Publishing (London, 2002)

Bidlingmaier, Gerhard, *Kriegsmarine Admiral Graf Spee*, ('Warship Profile 4'), Profile Publications (Windsor, 1971)

Breyer, Siegfried, *Battleships and Battlecruisers, 1905–1970*, Macdonald (London, 1973)

Brown, David, *Warship Losses of World War Two*, Arms and Armour Press (London, 1990)

Chesneau, Roger (ed.), *Conway's All the World's Fighting Ships, 1922–1946*, Conway Maritime Press (London, 1980)

Danielewicz, Waldemar, and Skwiot, Miroslaw, *Deutschland/Lützow* ('Monografie Morskie 7'), AJ Press (Gdynia, 1997)

——, *Admiral Graf Spee, Admiral Scheer* ('Monografie Morskie 8'), AJ Press (Gdansk, 1998)

Danielewicz, Waldemar, and Skwiot, Tadeusz, *Deutschland/Lützow, Admiral Graf Spee, Admiral Scheer* ('Monografie Morskie 9'), AJ Press (Gdansk, 1999)

Gröner, *German Warships 1815–1945. Vol 1: Major Surface Vessels*, Conway Maritime Press (London, 1990)

Hodges, Peter, *The Big Gun*, Conway Maritime Press (London, 1981)

Koop, Gerhard, and Schmolke, Klaus-Peter, *Pocket Battleships of the Deutschland Class*, Greenhill Books (London, 2000)

——, *Panzerschiffe der Deutschland-Klasse: Eine Bild- und Plandokumentation*, Bernard und Graefe (Bonn, 1993) Greenhill Books (London, 2000)

Pope, Dudley, *The Battle of the River Plate*, Chatham Publishing (London, 1999)

Roskill, Capt S. W., *The War at Sea* (3 vols), HMSO (London, 1954–61)

Rohwer, J., and Hummelchen, G., *Chronology of the War at Sea: The Naval History of World War Two*, Greenhill Books (London, 1992)

Whitley, M. J., *German Capital Ships of World War Two*, Arms and Armour Press (London, 1997)

PLANS

Vth Verlag für Technik und Handwerk GmbH, Robert-Bosch-Str. 4, D-76532 Baden-Baden, Germany

VIDEOS

DD Videos: DD 993 *Victory at Sea, Vol. 2*. Includes footage relating to *Admiral Graf Spee*.

DD Videos: DD 3188 *The German Imperial Navy 1919–1935*. The rebuilding of the German Navy between the wars.

WEBSITES (Specialist)

http://aumodelisme.hypermart.net/P/RALTABLE.HTM (for colour chip comparisons)

http://www.grafspee.com

http://www.warships1.com (photographs and specifications of all three *Panzerschiffe*)

http://www.geocities.com/Pentagon/Quarters/5768/ex_dtschl1.html (*Deutschland/Lützow*)

http://www.geocities.com/Pentagon/Quarters/5768/scheer1.html (*Admiral Scheer*)

http://www.geocities.com/Pentagon/Quarters/5768/spee1.html (*Admiral Graf Spee*)

http://www.waffenhq.de/schiffe/deutschlandklasse.html

http://www.deutschemarine.de/made/dmbas.nsf/DocName/themen_marine_geschichte_ReichsKriegsmarine_PanzerschiffA.htm (*Deutschland*)

http://www.deutsche-kriegsschiffe.de (pages for all three ships)

WEBSITES (General/modelling)

http://www.shipcamouflage.com
http://www.internetmodeler.com
http://www.modelwarships.com
http://warship.simplenet.com
http://smmlonline.com